When You Lose Someone You Love

∞

God Will Comfort You

Randy Petersen

Publications International, Ltd
Lincolnwood, IL 60712

ISBN-13: 978-1-4127-1527-0
ISBN-10: 1-4127-1527-X

Manufactured in U.S.A.

8 7 6 5 4 3 2 1

Randy Petersen is a freelance writer with more than 40 books to his credit, including *Bible Fun Stuff, The Family Book of Bible Fun, Praying Together, Why Me, God?,* and *100 Fascinating Bible Facts.* He is director of Bible education at a Methodist church in New Jersey.

Additional Contributors: Elaine Creasman, Christine A. Dallman, Margaret Anne Huffman, Marie D. Jones, Barbara Roberts Pine, Kimberly K. Smith, Natalie Walker Whitlock, Gary Wilde.

Cover Art: Art Beats; Brand X Pictures; Getty Images/Photo Disc.

Contents

The Truth About Grieving

*O*ver the centuries, many believers have turned to the Bible for comfort in their times of deepest need. When you lose someone you love, you desperately need some encouraging words. You might need to be reassured of God's love for you and for the person you're mourning. You might need permission to experience the overwhelming feelings of grief. Above all, you might need a heavenly perspective on these matters. As God sees it, death is *not* the end. He has a glorious eternity prepared for us. We find great consolation in these scriptural truths.

But there are different kinds of comfort—the gentle kind and the powerful kind. The gentle kind of comfort takes the form of quickly quoted phrases and loving pats. Someone might say, "Don't feel bad, because all things work together for good." This is true and often much needed. People want to show their concern for you, and these consolations are lovely gifts.

But sometimes you need a deeper comfort, a powerful comfort. You don't want to be told, "Don't feel bad," because you *do* feel bad, and you will for quite some time. What you need to hear is that God has not forgotten you, that he will embrace you in the most difficult times. You need to hear that you'll get through this pain—not around it, but through it—and that a new day will dawn at the end of this dark night of the soul.

You need to know that it's okay to cry. Hey, it's okay to holler and throw things. The loss of a loved one affects your entire self—your mind, your emotions, your body, and your spirit. But you *will* recover, in the proper time. You will not always understand why your loved one was taken; you don't need to. You need to hear that your muddled feelings don't make you a bad person, a weak believer, or a traitor to the loved one who's gone.

The great thing about the Bible is that it's both gentle and powerful. It gives us great assurances, but it doesn't sugarcoat the message. It tells us the truth about God— that we won't always understand him, but we can receive his amazing love. "My ways are above your ways," he tells us. He is beyond us but also beside us.

I pray that this book will be a source of both gentle and powerful comfort to you. It won't answer all your questions or even try to. I aim to tell you the truth about grieving—good, bad, and in between. And I want to open up the Scriptures in a way that will reveal the message of divine power and love.

—Randy Petersen

Blessed

Blessed are those who mourn, for they will be comforted.

—Matthew 5:4

*H*ave you seen the musical *Annie*? Based on the long-running comic strip "Little Orphan Annie," this story follows an abandoned child from the orphanage to the mansion of the richest man in the country—Daddy Warbucks. Annie even gets to tag along with him to a Cabinet meeting at the White House, where President Roosevelt's advisors are moaning about the Great Depression.

He gives power to the faint, and strengthens the powerless.

—Isaiah 40:29

It's a very cute scene. These experts are worried about poverty and unemployment and war—and rightly so. It was a bleak time. But then Annie starts singing, "The sun'll come out tomorrow." Her optimism is a hard sell in this smoke-filled room, but soon it inspires the president. He forces his reluctant advisors to sing along with Annie about the beauty of Tomorrow, Tomorrow.

The tide turns. Once the song is over, they all get back to work, but now they're looking at a bright future. The government could hire unemployed people, someone suggests, to do various projects that would keep America great. The ideas are flying fast and furious. FDR himself is agog at the possibilities. This is a new direction for the country, a way out of the doldrums. It's a New Deal.

And so the plucky optimism of a red-haired orphan changed the course of history. At least that's how the musical goes.

Cheerleaders

You probably know some people like Annie. When everything's looking grim, they're crowing about maintaining a positive mental outlook. Why so glum, chum? It will all work out, they say. Sure, you've had some hard times, but life will get better. Tomorrow's a new day. Cheer up. Let a smile be your umbrella. Turn that frown upside down.

O Lord, calm the waves of this heart; calm its tempests! Calm thyself, O my soul, so God is able to repose in thee, so that his peace may cover thee!... (L)et us know the truth of thy promise: that the world may not be able to take away thy peace.

——Søren Kierkegaard, *The Oxford Book of Prayer*

11

O let him, whose sorrow
No relief can find,
Trust in God, and borrow
Ease for the heart and mind.
Where the mourner weeping
Sheds the secret tear,
God His watch is keeping,
Though none else be near.
God will never leave thee,
All thy wants He knows,
Feels the pains that grieve thee,
Sees thy cares and woes.
Raise thine eyes to Heav'n
When thy spirits quail,
When, by tempests driven,
Heart and courage fail
All our woe and sadness,
In this world below,
Balance not the gladness
We in Heaven shall know.

—Book of Common Prayer,
Church of England

Chances are, those people really annoy you.

They mean well. They really do. But they're ignoring
a major truth about our existence. *Sometimes life hurts.*
It's like they're trying to slap a coat of bright, shiny
paint over any smudge of pain or sorrow. Sometimes you
even get the feeling that they're not trying to comfort
you at all. No, they're comforting *themselves.* They're
not paying attention to your emotional needs, but to their
own. Your sorrow bothers them—maybe it even scares
them a little—so they try to gloss over it. *But you need to
grieve.*

*After you bow your head in mourning,
lift your head in faith.*

The best comforters listen to you. They let you talk about how bad you feel. Yes, you need to talk about it sometimes. And there are other times when they'll sit with you in silence or share your tears. They may inject a note of hope every so often when you start despairing, but they're not about to burst into song. These people are gems. Treasure them. Keep them close beside you as you go through this difficult time. They may even help you fend off the annoying Annies.

I lift up my eyes to the hills—from where will my help come?

—Psalm 121:1

But if you find yourself surrounded by would-be cheerleaders who won't rest until you're singing "Tomorrow" along with them, just smile and thank them for their good wishes. The problem is, you're in no

condition to fight with them. You have a right to cry. You
have a *need* to cry. You just don't have the energy to fight
for it. They burst in with their perky pep talks and what
can you say? They seem to have the moral high ground.
Sometimes they can even make you feel that you're
unspiritual because you're not happy enough. When
you're already feeling down, that can drive you even
deeper into the pits.

But are they right? Doesn't God want us to "rejoice
always"? Let's take a look at what Jesus had to say.

> *Let nothing disturb thee;*
> *Let nothing dismay thee;*
> *All things pass;*
> *God never changes.*
> *Patience attains*
> *All that it strives for.*
> *He who has God*
> *Finds he lacks nothing.*
> *God alone suffices.*
>
> —St. Teresa of Avila

Lucky You

It was one of his first public statements, in a collection of sayings we know as the Beatitudes, at the beginning of the talk we call the Sermon on the Mount. The fact that this sermon appears in slightly different forms in the gospels of Matthew and Luke makes us think that Jesus preached it repeatedly. This was important material.

"Blessed are..."

That's how he begins each of his first nine sentences. The word *blessed* here means happy, fortunate, even lucky. It's really not a very religious term. Who are the

O God, help us not to despise or
oppose what we do not understand.

—William Penn

lucky people in this world? The rich? The powerful?
Those adored by millions or just cherished by their
own families? We all have our own opinions as to what
constitutes fortune. But Jesus proceeds to turn these ideas
upside down.

I'm in despair, God.
I'm in the black valley of hopelessness.
Please remind me that you are there
for me, even in my darkest hour.

My loved one has left me.
I know that person is now with you,
but I still miss him.
My grief is sometimes overwhelming—
Please help me remember that you are
here with me.

In all my pain, I sometimes forget that
you are here for me.
Remind me of your love.

Thank you, God.
Amen

The first lucky people he mentions are the "poor in spirit"; this would have shocked his listeners. Not the spiritual leaders. Not those who are confident in their ability to live righteous lives. No, it's the humble folk who are truly lucky—those who feel clumsy when it comes to spiritual matters. They are fortunate because God's kingdom belongs to them.

Comfort, dear God, those whose eyes are filled with tears and those whose backs are near breaking with the weight of a heavy burden. Heal those whose hearts hold a wound and whose faith has been dealt a blow. Bless all who mourn and who despair. Help those who can't imagine how they'll make it through another day. For your goodness and mercy are enough for all the troubles in the world. Amen.

Dear Lord,

I'm in pain.
Will I ever feel joy again?
I know I want this pain to go
away,
But I know I must feel this grief
to fully heal.

Give me peace and strength to
get through this difficult time.
Give me patience with this
process.
Give me patience with myself.
Give me patience with those
around me who are uncomfort-
able with my pain.
Give me your love, which can
sustain me.

Thank you, Lord.
Amen

We could dig into that first Beatitude for quite a while, but let's zero in on the second instead. *"Blessed are those who mourn."* Not the smiley faces. Not those who bravely soldier on as if nothing happened. When people suffer a great loss, they need to mourn. They need to weep for weeks, if that's what it takes. They need to fall apart at the seams. They need to feel as if they can't go on. Jesus says people are lucky if they mourn.

Why? Modern psychology gives us one answer. When you hold back your true feelings, you do damage to yourself. Keeping a stiff upper lip sounds like a great

> *All the words that I gather,*
> *And all the words that I write,*
> *Must spread out their wings untiring,*
> *And never rest in flight,*
> *Till they come where your sad, sad heart is,*
> *And sing to you in the night,*
> *Beyond where the waters are moving,*
> *Storm darkened or starry bright.*
> —William Peter Yates

plan, but it hurts you in the long run—both physically and emotionally. Our feelings were made to come out, and when we bottle them up, it puts great stress on our hearts, nerves, and immune systems. Some people (especially men, but not exclusively) are taught from childhood to hold back emotions such as sorrow and grief. It can be very therapeutic for such people to learn to let it out. Those who know how to mourn are the lucky ones.

But Jesus gives us a different answer. Mourners are blessed because "they will be comforted." There is something in the act of comforting that is good for us.

I believe in some blending of hope and sunshine sweetening the worst lots. I believe that this life is not all; neither the beginning nor the end. I believe while I tremble; I trust while I weep.

—Charlotte Brontë, *Villette*

New Connections

You may already be experiencing this. Perhaps there's someone who has stepped forward to help you in your time of grief. You now have a better, deeper relationship with this person. In some cases it's surprising who steps forward. Maybe someone you wouldn't expect has become an important friend in this time. Often it's someone who has recently experienced a loss and knows that pain firsthand. A new connection is created as these difficult emotions are shared.

This present sadness is so overwhelming that the rest of the story is forgotten, O God. Give me eyes of faith to read between the lines and see rebuilders, friends, and family, change and healing.

God,

How long will this grief last?
Shouldn't I feel better by now?
People tell me to get on with my life,
but I'm still full of sadness about my
loss.

Please, God, help me understand my
pain.
Give my aching heart rest.
Show me that your comfort is
available to me.

Thank you for your love and
assurance.

Amen

"How very good and pleasant it is when kindred live together in unity!" sings a psalmist (Psalm 133:1). That sounds wonderful, but the truth is, our world can be quite isolating at times. Everyone fends for himself or herself. People keep their deepest needs private. Sometimes it feels as if we live in little cubicles, never fully connecting with anyone. But the act of mourning and being comforted breaks down those barriers, as people reach out to help. As a result, we can all enjoy

Dear Lord,

My prayer is simple today.
I grieve, and I hurt.
Give me the strength to feel all this pain.

I sometimes feel that I can't survive it,
but I know that with your love and help,
I can.

Thank you for your abiding love.
Amen

those "good and pleasant" relationships the psalmist is lauding.

But it's not just other people who comfort us when we mourn. We also receive comfort from God. Paul calls him "the God of all consolation, who consoles us in all our affliction" (2 Corinthians 1:3–4). We were just exploring the deeper relationships that come from the comfort we receive from other people. The same is certainly true with God. In our time of deepest sorrow, we fall into his arms. We are emptied of all our pretense. Any hint of phony religion or proud posturing is gone. We simply have nothing left. And God meets us there.

He heals the broken-hearted, and
binds up their wounds.

—Psalm 147:3

The act of mourning cuts through a lot of our normal game-playing with God. When we experience the devastating grief of a major loss, we are reduced to the level of need. We have no gift to bring to the altar this time. We just crawl before the Lord and cry.

He embraces us. He gives us the strength to put one foot in front of the other. He stirs our emotions so they can heal properly. He brings caring people around us. In the process, we learn to trust him more and more. Our relationship deepens.

That seems to be Jesus' main point in all these Beatitudes. The lucky ones are not the rich and proud but the poor and needy. Why?

Because they have the amazing experience of relying on God for their daily sustenance, their future hope, and their ongoing comfort.

So don't feel bad for feeling bad. Jesus blessed your grief. You have enough to deal with right now without feeling guilty for grieving. You don't have to "cheer up." The sun may not come out tomorrow. In fact, your forecast is likely to be "party cloudy" for several more months. Grieving takes time.

But even as you feel the deep sorrow of your loss, you can appreciate those friends who sit beside you and hold your hand. You can deepen friendships with those who weep with you. And you can slowly become aware that the God of consolation is wrapping you in his loving embrace.

In the midst of mourning life's troubles,
you come to us. In the darkness, your
spirit moves, spreading light like a shower
of stars against a stormy night sky.

A Time to Heal

For everything there is a season, and a time for every matter under heaven... a time to mourn, and a time to dance.

—Ecclesiastes 3:1, 4

*Y*ou don't want to admit it at first. You want to pretend that everything is the same as it always was. When you lose someone you love, you know they're gone, but you still expect them to walk through the door at any moment.

Even when your mind has grasped the reality of this loss, your instincts are still lagging behind. You find yourself setting a place at the table for them or planning what you'll give them for Christmas. Especially in the first month or two, there are many heartbreaking moments as you remind yourself again and again of your loss.

They say when someone has had a limb amputated, they still feel phantom pains or itches from the missing part. It's a trick of the nervous system. The neural pathways are so deeply ingrained that it's hard to shut them down. Apologies for that stark word-picture, but losing a cherished loved one is much the same thing. That person has become a part of you. Your life has interacted with their life so intensely that you still feel as if they're just in the next room.

The experts call this *denial,* and it's normal. You might see it as a protective measure God has wired within us. When real life gets too painful, we ignore it for a while. You might be tempted

The best thing about the future is that
it comes only one day at a time.

—Abraham Lincoln

to scold yourself for this, but don't. You might be tempted to wonder: "What's wrong with me? Am I going crazy? Am I losing touch with reality?"

Relax. It's all part of a regular process of dealing with bad situations. God has allowed our minds to ease into these harsh circumstances. Denial is a temporary gift designed for our protection.

How long should you experience denial? That varies. Some losses are harder to take than others. Let's just say it's generally a matter of months rather than years. There are stories of parents who have been so devastated by the loss of a child that, for years afterward, they refused to change anything in the child's room. That's not healthy. At a certain point—months rather than years—you need to accept your loss and move forward in your life.

There is a natural process of recovery, and it usually starts with denial. But you don't need to follow any sort of schedule. Most people experience denial as long as they need to. When it's not helpful anymore, they naturally move on. Yet, occasionally, people get stuck in denial. They might need a helpful nudge from a pastor or counselor.

Yet, in the maddening maze of things,
And tossed by storm and flood,
To one fixed trust my spirit clings;
I know that God is good!...

I know not where His islands lift
Their fronded palms in air;
I only know I cannot drift
Beyond His love and care.

—— John Greenleaf Whittier, "The Eternal Goodness"

Mad About You

A second stage in this process is *anger.* Some people get
stuck here too, while others try to rush through it. Just
like denial, anger has a job to do. It's an important step in
a God-given process.

Many of us have trouble with anger in general. We
all feel it, but we differ broadly in how we express it.
Some are volcanoes, spewing out angry feelings and
then moving on as if nothing happened. Others are slow
cookers, stewing in hurt feelings for days or weeks
before letting anything out. Many religious folks feel

*In the depth of winter, I finally learned that
within me there lay an invincible summer.*

—Albert Camus

guilty when they get angry, so they try to hide those feelings. But the feelings are there, and they will find a way to come out, in healthful or unhealthful ways.

When you finally face the reality that you've lost someone close to you, it's natural to feel angry. But at whom? For what? It's not always clear. That's what makes this anger so tough to deal with.

*You need not cry very loud: he is
nearer to us than we think.*

—Brother Lawrence

Have you ever had a bad day when you were ready to lash out at anyone and everyone for the slightest problem? You were a bundle of anger looking for a reason to exist. That's sort of like the anger involved in the grieving process. You may not be sure what you're angry about, but you know something is wrong and you're upset. You feel a pain that you don't deserve. Someone ought to pay for that! And so you might let your anger out in a scattershot manner, holding grudges for silly things, taking offense at any raised eyebrow, and barking at everyone around you. Or you might focus it all on one poor soul who doesn't really deserve it. Then again, you might turn it on yourself.

He has sent me to ... bind
up the broken-hearted.

—Isaiah 61:1

You might be angry with *yourself* for not seeking the best medical care for the departed. You might scold yourself for things you said—or left unsaid. You might be mad at yourself for not spending more time with them.

*I know that at times I will be troubled, I know
that at times I will be belabored, I know that at
times I will be disquieted, but I believe that
I will not be overcome.*

—Julian of Norwich

You might be angry at *friends and relatives* for
not helping out enough with the funeral or other
arrangements or for not being there in those dying days.
You might be angry with the staff at the hospital or the
nursing home or the funeral home.

You might even be angry with *the loved one you lost*.
This can be especially difficult. You feel it, but you
don't want to admit it. It seems wrong to dishonor
their memory with such complaints, but this feeling
festers within you. They never got around to buying life
insurance. They left you out of the will. Or maybe their

When You Lose Someone You Love

death was largely their own fault, through smoking or drinking or not seeing a doctor. *If only you weren't so stubborn, you'd still be here today!*

Ultimately, many people feel angry with *God.* This is often the hardest to admit. We believe in a loving God who wants what's best for us, right? Then how could he allow us to feel so much pain? This is especially true if your loved one has been taken in the prime of life. It seems *wrong,* and God should be held responsible for that. Shouldn't he? When feeling this type of anger, many people begin living double lives, spiritually. They act as if they're on great terms with God, but they're secretly holding a serious grudge. As a result, they find it hard to pray like they used to.

Honest Anger

What can you do with your anger? First, *don't feel guilty about it.* It's just another part of the recovery process.

36

I awoke at dawn one morning
From a restless night of sorrow,
Praying that with the daylight
Might come a bright tomorrow.
My heart as cold and hopeless
As winter's deepest chill,
I cried out for understanding
And to know my Father's will.
While treading up a garden path
Hushed in the fragrant air;
I spied a tender rose,
Its petals bowed as if in prayer.
As I gazed in silent awe,
It occurred to me—He knows!
The tears my Lord has shed for me
Are the dew upon the rose.

Like denial, it's an important but temporary step toward healing.

Be honest in your anger. Think about a couple's first date. They dress nicer than they normally dress; they act nicer than they normally act; they show more interest than they normally show—all in the hopes of finding someone who will love them as they really are. That relationship might start as a surface attraction, but if it's going to grow, they'll both need to develop more honesty.

When someone passes away, the community of family and friends usually honors their memory by focusing on

My Creator, I know in my heart that these tears will one day give way again to joy, yet for now I know only pain. Help me find the courage to let these tears flow, to feel the loss and heartbreak, so that I may come out whole and cleansed again. For on the other side of my sorrow I know life waits for me. I want to laugh again.

the good things rather than the bad. But you need to get past that surface level if you're going to develop a lasting relationship with the memory of this loved one. You have to get honest. It might seem disrespectful to scold this person after they've passed, but it could be your way of saying what needs to be said. In a way you're saying, "I want to treasure your memory as the person you really were, not some phony, airbrushed image."

The same thing might be said about God. You might feel funny about scolding God, but there's a rich biblical tradition of people who did just that. Moses was great at it. David wrote the book of Psalms for that purpose. If

Why are you cast down, O my soul, and why are you disquieted within me? Hope in God; for I shall again praise him, my help and my God.

—Psalm 42:11

you want to get past the first-date stage with God, you have to be honest. Tell him how you really feel—and then listen for how he feels. If there's anger involved, that's not a problem. God can take it.

Be careful about fallout. Of course the problem with anger is that it can do damage. If you lash out in anger against everyone who crosses your path, you'll hurt a lot of feelings, destroy some relationships, and maybe even cause injury. So look for harmless ways to unfurl your angry energy. One woman bought a set of old dishes at a yard sale and took them out to the woods. Then she hurled those dishes at the trees, smashing them to bits,

He has made everything suitable for its time;
moreover, he has put a sense of past and
future into their minds.

—Ecclesiastes 3:11

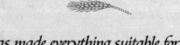

Creator God,

I know you created me, all of me. You made my laughter, but also my tears. You crafted the processes of my heart and mind. You know when I need to come face-to-face with reality, and you know when I can only deal with it in small doses. You understand me better than I do.

The truth is, I'm confused sometimes by my own behavior. I try to be positive, but then I'm crying my eyes out. I try to have a good cry, and I end up irritated over silly things. I try to vent my anger, and I feel guilty about that. And then I feel guilty for feeling guilty.

This is a difficult road I'm on, Lord. I ask that you travel it with me. Hold me close. I'm not asking you to cheer me up all the time, just let me know that you're beside me, behind me, guiding me along. I don't need to see where all this is leading; I just need to know that today I'm a step beyond where I was yesterday. Can you go with me step by step?

Thank you, my loving Lord. Amen.

while hollering at everyone with whom she was angry. One man used his angry energy to tackle some cleaning projects in his home he'd been avoiding for years.

Some people get stuck in anger. Again, it should last for months, not years. But in most cases the anger subsides when it needs to.

Quick Fixes and Pit Stops

Experts call the next stage *bargaining,* but that can be confusing. It might be better to speak of this part of the process as "quick fixes." This is when you try something rash to ease the pain. Some people make vows to God at this point: *If you get me through this, I will become a missionary.* Some who have lost their mates suddenly get remarried, expecting that the joy of their new union will ease their sorrow. (Sometimes that works, but usually it puts extra strain on the new relationship.)

Those who wait for the Lord shall renew their
strength, they shall mount up with wings like eagles,
they shall run and not be weary, they shall walk
and not faint.

—Isaiah 40:31

This is also the time when various addictions come to the surface. If you've ever struggled with drugs or alcohol, you will be tempted to salve your pain with those substances. People also throw themselves into gambling, shopping, eating, exercising, or even video games. These are all attempts at quick fixes.

So don't be surprised when these temptations emerge. Be ready for them. The truth is, these quick fixes won't solve anything. At best, they're distractions. At worst, they're destructions. You might even want to have a friend on call, someone who can hold you accountable and keep you from doing something you'll regret later.

The only way out of the pain is *through* it. Keep moving through the process. Unfortunately, the next stage is the pits—specifically, the pit of *depression*. When you finally realize there's nothing you can do, the full reality of your loss comes crashing down on you. The sadness hits. You get weepy. You get lethargic. You can't taste your food. You don't care about the things you used to enjoy. You don't sleep well. You go through your days in a haze.

So you have pain now; but I will see you again, and your hearts will rejoice, and no one will take away your joy from you.

—John 16:22

This is when the people around you start trying to cheer you up—and you just want them to go away. *It's been six months since the funeral. Isn't it time you got over it?* Frankly, they don't know what they're talking about. You need to spend some time in the pits. It's the way you heal.

So we do not lose heart...our inner nature is being renewed day by day.

—2 Corinthians 4:16

If you were to break an arm, the doctors would put it in a cast, immobilizing it so the bone could heal properly. It's the same thing when your heart gets broken with grief. Your emotions will naturally go into depression— immobilizing them—so they can heal properly. It takes time. If you rush it, you'll probably sink back into depression at a later time. You will be frustrated by it.

Lord of second chances,

Just when I thought I had this handled, I slipped back. I was feeling almost healthy again. I actually cracked a smile, I think. After months of heartache, that's really something. For a moment I envisioned a future—yes, a future without the one I've lost, but a future full of precious memories. It was there, in front of me, almost within reach . . . and then I got upset again, and the tears were flowing, and I was saying and thinking things I didn't want to say or think. I'm not sure what happened.

Lord, I ask you to cover me with your love. Let your Spirit fill my heart. Whisper your assurances to me every day. Give me another chance to put my heart back together. Calm the hurricane that rages inside of me.

And please be patient with me. I'm likely to stir up a new storm as soon as you've soothed the old one. These days I'm celebrating every step forward by taking two steps back. I need your power in my life, pulling me forward. Restore the joy of your salvation.

I ask this humbly. Amen.

You will want the depression to be over and done with. And then one day it will be.

Unveiling

There's a wise tradition in the Jewish faith. One year after someone dies, their tombstone is unveiled in a ceremony that marks the end of an official mourning period. Of course this doesn't mean that all sadness is over, but it's a helpful way to turn a page in your life, to focus on living rather than dying.

As psychology experts have studied the recovery process over the last half-century—denial, anger, quick fixes, and depression—they have found that it usually takes about a year. There are exceptions to this, naturally, and certain factors that might extend or shorten the time, but you can expect a year or so of emotional downtime. It's God's way of "restoring our soul."

Joy Comes with the Morning

*Weeping may linger for the night, but
joy comes with the morning.*

—Psalm 30:5

*A*fter losing a loved one, you may feel that you're wandering in a fog. Passing through denial, anger, and various attempts at quick fixes to escape the pain, you settle into the bitter reality. You can't escape the truth. You have suffered a major loss, and you're not sure how you'll go on.

*God be praised, that to believing souls, gives
light in darkness, comfort in despair.*

—William Shakespeare

Depression saps you of energy. You might prefer to stay in bed all day, but sleep is elusive. Your senses are dimmed. Nothing seems to matter very much, not even the basic elements of daily life. As the psalmist puts it: "My tears have been my food day and night" (42:3).

*May those who sow in tears reap
with shouts of joy. Those who go
out weeping, bearing the seed for sowing,
shall come home with shouts of joy,
carrying their sheaves.*

—Psalm 126:5–6

Then one day you wake up and smell the coffee. Literally.

One day you'll notice the sun shining a bit brighter, your breakfast tasting a bit sweeter, your shower feeling a bit warmer. It's as if the fog has lifted, the veil drawn away. You are ready to live again.

It happens differently for different people. For some, it comes through the care and convincing of others: "You know, you're right. I do need to get over this."

For others, it's a sort of arbitrary line in the sand they step across: "It has been a year now. Time to rejoin the human race."

You grew weary from your many wanderings, but you did not say, "It is useless." You found your desire rekindled, and so you did not weaken.

—Isaiah 57:10

Others might dare to try some activity that draws them out of themselves: "I thought I'd hate square dancing, but it was actually kind of fun."

But for many, many people, it just happens without warning or impetus. Little by little, step by step, time begins to heal their wounds.

Lord,
Just help me hang on. Help me get through. Help me put one foot in front of the other. Help me do what I have to do for those who rely on me. I don't even know how I'm going to get through. I can't see past today's pain. I feel like giving up. But I trust you to help me. I trust you to give me the strength I need.

And it's all I can do to say, Amen.

A year after her husband died, a widow surprised a friend by suddenly saying, "I think I'm ready now. I'm ready to date again. I need someone to hug." A week earlier, maybe even an *hour* earlier, she would not have been ready. But at that moment she knew: Her long night of weeping was over. She was finished with her depression and ready to get on with her life.

As stated about the other stages of grief, you just need a certain amount of time for your system to restore. When you're ready to move from one stage to the next, you

Then shall the young women rejoice in the dance,
and the young men and the old shall be merry. I will
turn their mourning into joy, I will comfort them,
and give them gladness for sorrow.

—Jeremiah 31:13

*Once, in my imagination I was taken
down to the bed of the sea, and
saw there green hills and dales that seemed
to be clothed with moss, seaweed
and stones. And I understood that
if a person firmly believes that
God is always with man,
then even if he is thrown into the
depths of the sea, he will be
preserved in body and soul, and
will enjoy greater solace and
comfort than all this world can offer.*

—— Julian of Norwich, *Revelations of Divine Love*

will. There's no value in rushing through it, because you'll slip back later. Grief is a piper you have to pay, sooner or later. But this also means you don't need to worry as you go through the process. You are not abnormal when you feel sudden anger, odd temptations, or paralyzing depression. And when the time is right, you will move on.

God of all comfort,
 I miss this dear one I've lost. I've been through the questions and tears. I know all things work together, but now it just comes down to missing. I want them here with me now, and I know that can't happen. I miss them, and now it feels like a piece of me is missing.
 Restore me, please. Make me whole again. Bring comfort to my heart.

Amen.

Friday Faith

The story is told of a preacher who stood up in church and said, "It's Friday, but Sunday's coming!" He got a few "Amens" from the faithful, and he repeated, "It's Friday, but Sunnnnday's coming!" The response got a little bigger, and he said it again.

Only by moving through the pain
do we get to embrace the gift
of healing and call it our own.

Soon the whole church was rocking with "That's right" and "Hallelujah," as people caught on to his message. "It's Friday," he said, and the parishioners understood the tragedy of Jesus on the cross. "But Sunday's coming,"

*O Holy Creator, who hath bound
together heaven and Earth, let me
walk through your kingdom comforted
and protected by the warm rays
of your love. Let me be healed as
I stand basking in the divine light
of your presence, where strength
and hope and joy are found.
Let me sit at rest in the
valley of your peace, surrounded
by the fortress of your loving care.*

and they knew the glory of the empty tomb was not far away. "It's Friday," he kept saying, and they saw the sadness of their own lives as the momentary grief of the disciples mourning the loss of their Lord. "But Sunnnnday is coming!" And they knew that there was a resurrection morning ahead for them as well.

As the story goes, that was the entire sermon in church that day, and it was surely the most memorable. Those listeners were reminded that God's specialty is turning tragedy to triumph, that our grimmest griefs are transformed into God's greatest glories.

Let this be your comfort: You are not the first to walk in the fearful path nor will you be the last. But each traveler is precious to God and walks under his watchful eyes.

The Word from the Pit

David had a similar truth in mind as he penned Psalm
30. "O Lord my God, I cried to you for help, and you
have healed me. O Lord, you . . . restored me to life from
among those gone down to the Pit" (vs. 2–3).

Even in the midst of grieving,
the mourner sooner or later
begins to see little
glimmers of hope.
First an hour will go by
when he does not think of his loss,
then a few hours,
then a day. Slowly,
reconstruction begins.

—Billy Graham

Interesting choice of words there. For David, the Pit was death. He might be saying, "I almost died in battle, and you, Lord, saved my life." But this is a psalm about mourning, not about warfare. It's quite possible that he was mourning over the death of others and feeling a depression that was almost as if he himself were dying.

Before becoming king, David spent quite a while on the run from a jealous King Saul. One priest who helped David was later brutally murdered by Saul's forces. Perhaps David was mourning the loss of this courageous friend and feeling guilty about putting him in harm's way.

When it is dark enough, you can see the stars.

—Ralph Waldo Emerson

David's best friend was Prince Jonathan, son of Saul. Both Saul and Jonathan died in the same battle, clearing the way for David to become king but causing him much sorrow as well.

As king, David had to fend off a revolt led by his son Absalom. David's top general killed the rebel prince, and David wept bitterly.

David also had an adulterous affair with Bathsheba, ordering her husband's death and conceiving a child with

*All human wisdom is summed up
in two words: wait and hope.*
——Alexandre Dumas, *The Count of Monte Cristo*

Lord, how can I endure this
life of sorrows, unless you
strengthen me with your mercy
and grace? Do not turn your
face from me. Do not withdraw
your consolation from me, lest my
soul becomes like a waterless desert.
Teach me, O Lord, to do your will,
and to live humbly. You alone know
me perfectly, seeing into my soul. You
alone can give lasting peace and joy.

—Thomas à Kempis

her. The prophet Nathan confronted David about the sin and predicted that the child would be stillborn. David publicly repented, clothing himself in ritual sackcloth, and he grieved for this loss.

For my part,
I will sing of your strength;
I will celebrate your love
in the morning; For you have
become my stronghold,
a refuge in the day
of my trouble.
To you, O my Strength, will I sing;
for you, O God, are my stronghold
and my merciful God.
—*Book of Common Prayer,* Church of England

Any one of these events could have sparked Psalm 30. David certainly knew about grief. "Weeping may linger for the night," he wrote, "but joy comes with the morning" (v. 5).

What's this? Joy? The psalms have a way of telling the beginning, middle, and end of a story all at once. In the following verses, David explains how his pride got him into trouble, how he cried out to the Lord, and how he tried to convince the Lord to come to his aid. But he blurts out the end of the story early—there is joy in the morning.

"You have turned my mourning into dancing," he added later. "You have taken off my sackcloth and clothed me with joy, so that my soul may praise you and not be silent" (vs. 11–12).

David never downplayed his troubled times. This was not denial on his part. He knew what it was like to weep all night and weep the next night, too. He faced more than his share of tragedy, some of which he brought on himself. But he understood that this story of grief had a happy ending. The night is long and difficult, but the day will dawn. And the new day will bring not only joy but dancing.

You may be in the middle of the grieving process. You might even be in that pit of depression. When you hear that joy comes with the morning, it might seem very far away. That's understandable. You don't need to do a joyful foxtrot yet; just know that it's in your future. It's still Friday for you, and you have plenty to grieve about. But Sunday's coming. And when that day dawns, you will dance.

Lord of joy,
    Joy! Now there's a word
I haven't considered for a
while. Joy? Is that possible?
After what I've been through,
could I ever feel your sweet
joy again? Survival, okay.
Maintenance, sure. I'm already slogging through each
day, and I thank you for that.
But joy? What bonfire will
you have to light in my heart
to make that happen? I can't
wait to see how you bring joy
to my morning.

    In humble faith, Amen.

Peace that Passes Understanding

And the peace of God, which surpasses all understanding,
will guard your hearts and your minds in Christ Jesus.

—Philippians 4:7

"*I* am sixty years old and for the first time during all these long years, so far as memory serves me, has God in his infinite mercy allowed me to have any sorrow that I could not cast on him."

...in all human sorrows nothing
gives comfort but love and faith.

— Leo Tolstoy, *Anna Karenina*

The writer of those words was William Booth, founder of the Salvation Army. His wife lay dying, and he couldn't understand why. Booth was a man of great faith. His preaching had brought challenge and comfort to thousands, but watching his beloved Catherine ebb away was "an experience of sorrow, which words can but poorly describe." He tried to go about his daily routine, rising at six, working for two hours before breakfast, but still he found himself breaking down in tears, moaning, "How can it be? How can it be?"

The Lord is good to those who wait
for him, to the soul that
seeks him. It is good that one
should wait quietly for
the salvation of the Lord.

—Lamentations 3:25–26

Maybe you are experiencing a similar grief. Along with the sorrow comes the question: "Why, God, why?" This usually makes the sorrow worse. At the very moment when you need to "cast your care" on your comforting Lord, you find yourself nurturing deep suspicions about his intentions. How could he let this happen?

> *Creator of all,*
>   *I see the surface of a lake, and it's so serene. The breeze wafts gently over the water. A dragonfly circles. Birds soar overhead. The scene calls me to a gentleness of spirit.*
>   *But as you know, my spirit has been anything but gentle lately. I've been wracked with questions, tormented by doubts, burning with anger. I long for your peace. Grant me your peace. Breathe into my life your gentle peace.*
>   *Amen*

Many people have an intellectual curiosity about this question. If God is all-loving and God is all-powerful, then how could he allow painful events to occur in our lives? Philosophers have considered this problem in one volume after another, but when a crisis hits home, suddenly it's more than a mental exercise. When we lose someone precious, it's an emotional issue. We tend to feel that God has betrayed us. And that creates another major loss in our lives—a loss of intimacy with our Creator, perhaps even a loss of faith.

All around, the storms may churn,
the seas may rage, the fires burn.
But deep within you, you will not fear,
you will have peace when centered there.
For even amidst the tempest wild,
God will be there to guide you, Child.

Feeling Betrayed

What do we do with that feeling of betrayal? People usually go in one of two directions. Some find their faith shattered. If they've trusted God to protect them and their loved ones from pain and harm, then they've been disappointed, to say the least. They feel that God has proven untrustworthy. Why should they continue to worship a God who either cannot help or doesn't care?

> *Lord God,*
>
> *"I am not skilled to understand what God has willed, what God has planned."*
>
> *I can relate to the words of that old hymn because I don't get it. Maybe if I had a theology degree I could figure something out, but honestly I'm clueless. I do not have the skill to understand why you would allow such pain and grief in my life.*
>
> *I trust you. I'm trying to trust you more. Can you help me out on this?*
>
> *Amen*

God hath not promised
Skies always blue,
Flower-strewn pathways
All our lives through;
God hath not promised
Sun without rain,
Joy without sorrow,
Peace without pain.
But God hath promised
Strength for the day.
Rest for the labor,
Light for the way,
Grace for the trials,
Help from above,
Unfailing sympathy,
Undying love.

—Annie Johnson Flint

This is strong language, to be sure, but these are strong feelings. After losing a loved one, many people get very angry with God, and they take it out on him by shutting him out of their lives. No more church. No more Bible. What's the use?

My Creator, blessed is your presence. For you and you alone give me power to walk through dark valleys into the light again. You and you alone give me hope when there seems no end to my suffering. You and you alone give me peace when the noise of my life overwhelms me. I ask that you give this same power, hope, and peace to all who know discouragement, that they, too, may be emboldened and renewed by your everlasting love. Amen.

The other direction is more pious but less honest. People feel hurt by God, but they don't want to admit that. They don't want to be disrespectful, so they don't tell God how they really feel. They pretend to continue in their faith, as if nothing happened—but their faith has actually been severely jolted. They end up holding a grudge against God and remaining very distant. It's sort of like that uncle who owes you money but won't pay up. You see him at family functions and you might even say hello in a terse, formal way, but there's a distance between you.

Both of these directions are understandable options. When your world has turned upside down, it's only natural to reappraise your faith. But there is a better way.

Be still, and know that I am God!

—Psalm 46:10

The Sufferer

The Book of Job raises similar questions. It starts out with a wager between God and the devil. God is actually bragging about Job's faith, and Satan suggests that it's only because God takes such good care of him. Job was, after all, a rich rancher with a large family. Why wouldn't he trust the God who gave all this to him?

So God agrees to let Satan take away Job's wealth and his family, and ultimately even his health. Despite all of that, Job refuses to curse God. His own wife mocks him on her way out the door, but Job responds, "Shall we receive the good at the hand of God, and not receive the bad?" (Job 2:10).

Job has three friends, and later a fourth, who come over and sit with him in his sorrow. The bulk of the book consists of their attempts to explain his suffering. Generally, they suggest that he must have done

O Lord, calm the waves of this heart;
calm its tempests. Calm thyself, O my soul,
so that the divine can set in thee.
Calm thyself, O my soul, so that
God is able to repose in thee,
so that his peace may cover thee.

Yes, Father in heaven, often have
we found that the world cannot give
us peace, O but make us feel that
thou art able to give peace; let us know
the truth of thy promise: that the whole
world may not be able to take away thy peace.

—Søren Kierkegaard, *The Oxford Book of Prayer*

something to deserve his suffering. Why else would God allow this to happen? Job doggedly maintains his innocence.

Finally God himself speaks, and we perk up, expecting answers. Instead, he brings more questions. "Can you make an ocean?" he asks. "I can." In highly poetic language, he surveys his creation. "Can you make a hippopotamus? I can. You see those stars? I put them there." This is a loose paraphrase, of course, but the gist of God's argument is this: "I'm God, and you're not."

> *Drop thy still dews of quietness,*
> *Till all our strivings cease;*
> *Take from our souls the strain and stress,*
> *And let our ordered lives confess*
> *The beauty of thy peace.*
> —John Greenleaf Whittier, *The Oxford Book of Prayer*

As Frederick Buechner puts it: "God doesn't explain. He explodes.... God doesn't reveal his grand design. He reveals himself." There's wisdom in that approach. As we look back over this Book of Job, we realize that it's not really about suffering; *it's about faith in the midst of suffering.* The wager is based on Job's faith. And what is Job's faith based on?

Well, if it was based on a set of answers to theological questions, he would be in trouble. That was apparently the situation with Job's friends—at least the first three. They trusted in their idea of how God should run things: good rewards for good behavior; consequences for bad behavior. That makes a lot of sense, and many people today share that basic idea. But God rises above that level. He refuses to be boxed in by our sense of what he should and shouldn't do. He keeps surprising us. After all, he's God and we're not.

Finding His Peace

What is your faith based on? Are you trusting in God or a set of ideas about God? Are you trusting in the Creator of all, whose ways are higher than your ways, whose thoughts are higher than your thoughts (Isaiah 55:9)? What kind of God would he be if he fit into our boxes?

If your faith has been shattered, or at least challenged, by the sorrowful events of the past—maybe that's a good thing. Maybe some of your ideas about God need to be reshaped. Maybe it's an opportunity to consider how great and awesome God is, how far beyond our expectations he resides.

> *Have thine own way, Lord! Have thine own way! Wounded and weary, help me I pray! Power, all power, surely is thine! Touch me and heal me, Savior divine!*
>
> — Adelaide A. Pollard, "Have Thine Own Way, Lord"

Does this mean that God doesn't love us? Not at all. But he certainly loves us in ways we don't always understand. A child may misunderstand a parent's intentions: *I have to leave my playmates and come inside for dinner? Now? You don't love me anymore!* Of course that's far from the truth. The parent loves the child in ways that are higher than the child's understandings.

Does this mean that God is always distant and awe-inspiring, rather than close and comforting? Not at all. God draws near to us in our need. He promises peace.

The apostle Paul was in prison when he wrote to the believers at Philippi, "Do not worry about anything, but in everything by prayer and supplication with thanksgiving let your requests be made known to God. And the peace of God, which surpasses all understanding, will guard your hearts and your minds in Christ Jesus" (Philippians 4:6–7).

Prayer is a cure for anxiety. The God who made the universe—oceans and stars and hippopotamuses—*wants* to hear about our problems. When we turn our anxieties, our frustrations, and our sorrows over to him, he gives us peace. But notice how he describes this peace. It "surpasses all understanding."

You might never understand why. Your questions might bubble up forever. As we saw in the case of Job, God tends not to give answers. But he does give himself. He brings his awesome, surprising presence into your life and wraps you up in his peace.

As he prepared to leave his disciples, Jesus said something similar. "Peace I leave with you; my peace I give to you. I do not give to you as the world gives. Do not let your hearts be troubled, and do not let them be afraid" (John 14:27). Notice again: His peace is not "as the world gives." People might expect answers to all questions. They might expect wealth and pleasure in reward for faithfulness. They might expect believers to get a free ride on matters of suffering. That's the world's kind of peace, but the Lord's peace is different. He sees us through our hard times. We don't need to have troubled hearts, not because we're immune from trouble, but because God is with us. We rest in him, and he grants us peace.

Lord,

I'm beginning to understand something. I've been pounding on the gates of heaven asking for—no, demanding: answers. Why? Why? Why? You had upset the even keel of my life, and I want to know the reason.

I still want to know the reason, but here's what I'm beginning to get. You never promised us answers. What you have promised us is peace. So that's what I'm asking for now. Give me answers when you're ready, but please give me peace as soon as possible, just as you promised.

Amen

I Am with You Always

And remember, I am with you always, to the end of the age.

—Matthew 28:20

*J*onathan Edwards was probably the most famous man in colonial America. Respected as a scholar, revered as a pastor, he finally reached the peak of his profession at age 54, when he was asked to serve as president of Princeton University (then known as the College of New Jersey). He left the pastorate of his Massachusetts church to assume this prestigious post. His wife, Sarah, was going to wrap things up at home and join him in New Jersey a few months later.

At least that was the plan. Just a few weeks into his new job, before Sarah could join him, Jonathan came down with smallpox. As he lay dying, he dictated this message: "Give my kindest love to my dear wife and tell her that the uncommon union that has so long subsisted between us has been ... spiritual and therefore will continue forever. And I hope she will be supported under so great a trial and submit cheerfully to the will of God. And as to my children, you are now ... left fatherless, which I hope will be an inducement to you to seek a Father who will never fail you."

Teach us to know, God, that it is exactly at the point of our deepest despair that you are closest. For at those times we can finally admit we have wandered in the dark, without a clue. Yet you have been there with us all along. Thank you for your abiding presence.

One of his grown daughters, who now lived in New Jersey, was at his bedside. But he would never see his wife and other children again. At least not on this side of eternity. His last words of wisdom to his daughter were: "Trust in God and you do not need to be afraid."

As you would expect, Sarah took the news hard. Not only was there the shock of losing her husband and the grief involved with that, but her mind was flooded with questions. Why would God lead Jonathan to this faraway job, only to let him die before he could get anything done? Surely Jonathan had more good work to do on this Earth. Why would God take him now? It just didn't make sense.

> *Prayer is the burden of a sigh,*
> *The falling of a tear,*
> *The upward glancing of an eye*
> *When none but God is near.*
> —James Montgomery

In the following weeks and months, she continued to wrestle with this issue. A woman of great faith, she didn't want to doubt God's goodness, but it was hard to trust in him after what had happened. Jonathan was well known for preaching about God's sovereignty, and Sarah had often helped him plan his sermons and writings. So we can assume that she thoroughly understood the theology of a God who is completely in charge, a God who can do whatever he wants. But that might have made it even harder for her to grasp this situation. Why would God do this to her?

For the mountains may depart and the hills be removed, but my steadfast love shall not depart from you, and my covenant of peace shall not be removed, says the Lord, who has compassion on you.

—Isaiah 54:10

Two weeks after Jonathan's death, Sarah wrote to one of her children: "What shall I say? A holy and good God has covered us with a dark cloud." She credits the goodness of God for the fact that "we had him so long." And in the midst of her sorrow, she adds, "But my God lives, and he has my heart. Oh, what a legacy my husband and your father has left us. We are all given to God and there I am and love to be."

Yes, I have doubted. I have wandered off the path. I have been lost. But I always returned. It is beyond the logic I seek. It is intuitive—an intrinsic, built-in sense of direction. I seem always to find my way home. My faith has wavered but has saved me.

—Helen Hayes

*Into the bleakest winters
of our souls, Lord, you are
tiptoeing on tiny infant feet to
find us. May we drop whatever we're doing and accept
this gesture of a baby so small
it may get overlooked in our
frantic search for something
massive and overwhelming.
Remind us that it is not you
who demands lavish celebra-
tions and strobe-lit displays
of faith. Rather, you ask only
that we have the faith of a
mustard seed and willingness
to let a small hand take ours.
We are ready.*

The Lord is my light and my salvation; whom shall I fear? The Lord is the stronghold of my life; of whom shall I be afraid? . . . For he will hide me in his shelter in the day of trouble; he will conceal me under the cover of his tent; he will set me high on a rock. . . . I believe that I shall see the goodness of the Lord in the land of the living. Wait for the Lord; be strong, and let your heart take courage; wait for the Lord!

——Psalm 27:1, 5, 13, 14

It's never easy. The death of a loved one puts anyone into an emotional and spiritual jumble. Sarah Edwards admitted that her life was covered with "a dark cloud," but reaffirmed her faith in a "holy and good God." You might not be so articulate, and you don't have to be. We saw the same sort of jumble in the psalms, great faith interspersed with bitter complaints and cries for help. *Where are you? Help me! Why do you allow this? I praise you. I need you. Thank you.* In the throes of grief, that emotional roller coaster ride is to be expected.

Let us therefore approach the throne of grace with boldness, so that we may receive mercy and find grace to help in the time of need.
—Hebrews 4:16

"My tears have been my food day and night," one psalmist complains, "while people say to me continually, "Where is your God?' " Later in the same composition, he asks God, "Why have you forgotten me?" (Psalm 42:3, 9).

I would rather walk with God in the dark
than go alone in the light.

— Mary Gardiner Brainard

Many believers feel hesitant to give voice to these questions, but there they are in the Bible! Even Jesus exclaimed from the cross, "My God, my God, why have you forsaken me?" (Matthew 27:46). There's nothing wrong with asking such questions—just don't let that be the end of the conversation. Jesus went on to say, "Father, into your hands I commend my spirit"

(Luke 23:46). And, as we've seen, the psalmist keeps us guessing. Taunted by his enemies, feeling totally forgotten by God, he does a bit of self-analysis. "Why are you cast down, O my soul, and why are you disquieted within me? Hope in God; for I shall again praise him, my help and my God" (Psalm 42:11). He's completely honest about his current state of mind, but he knows the final chapter hasn't been written yet.

> *God be in my head,*
> *and in my understanding;*
> *God be in my eyes,*
> *and in my looking;*
> *God be in my mouth,*
> *and in my speaking;*
> *God be in my heart,*
> *and in my thinking;*
> *God be at my end,*
> *and at my departing.*
>
> —Old Sarum Primer, *The Oxford*
> *Book of Prayer*

Where Is He?

So where is God when we need him?

Nearby.

He's like a dad teaching a kid to ride a bike. For a while he runs alongside, his hands firmly on the bike and the child. But at a certain point the hands come off, and the child rides alone. Where's Dad? Close behind, watching, maybe praying, ready to rush in if needed.

Or consider the toddler racing down the aisle in a supermarket. It's all about her feet, her new shoes, her teetering balance, and all the cool stuff on the bottom shelves. But suddenly she stops and looks around. Where's Mom? Suddenly her sense of adventure is replaced by paralyzing fear. Of course Mom is only a few steps away, moving in quickly to scoop up the crying youngster. But those few seconds seem like forever in the child's young experience. And the tears are as much about anger as fear. "Where were you, Mom? Why weren't you there when I needed you? You left me out there, all alone, for four, maybe even five seconds! How could you?"

O Lord, you have searched me
and known me. You know when I
sit down and when I rise up; you
discern my thoughts from far away.
You search out my path and my
lying down, and are acquainted
with all my ways. Even before a
word is on my tongue, O Lord, you
know it completely. You hem me
in, behind and before, and lay your
hand upon me.

—Psalm 139:1–5

We do the same sort of thing with God. We feel abandoned in a time of great need. We're afraid and angry. But the truth is, he's right there with us. We may not recognize him right away. He might be allowing us to move out on our own a little, but he's never far.

Lord,

Forgive me for forgetting. I know you're with me "always." You have said it in a hundred Bible verses. "Fear not, for I am with you." Even in the "valley of the shadow of death," you are with me. I know all that, but I forget to look for you. I cry out in pain as if no one's listening, but you are right there beside me. You do care about me.

So, I'm sorry for my selective memory. I trust in your forgiveness.

Amen

"Do not fear," the Lord said through Isaiah, "for I am with you, do not be afraid, for I am your God; I will strengthen you, I will help you, I will uphold you with my victorious right hand" (Isaiah 41:10). The author of Hebrews seconded this motion. "For he has said, 'I will never leave you or forsake you' " (Hebrews 13:5).

And the Word became flesh and lived among us.

——John 1:14

It is part of God's nature to be with us. In the Garden of Eden, God came looking for Adam and Eve even after they had sinned (Genesis 3:9). In a time of national threat, God gave Isaiah a specific message to console his people. A child would be born with the Hebrew title *Emmanuel,* "God with us" (Isaiah 7:14). That prophecy was later applied to the miraculous birth of Jesus, who

95

was called the Word (of God) that "became flesh and lived among us" (Matthew 1:23; John 1:14).

God has never chosen to be a distant overlord who winds up his creation and lets it run on its own. The entire Bible is the record of his involvement with his people. He acts in human history. He talks with people. He motivates people to make a difference. He longs for a deeper relationship with humankind. Yes, there have been times when Moses or David or Jeremiah wondered where God had gone. Situations had grown so bad that the Lord seemed absent. But the truth, as they eventually acknowledged, was that God was never far away.

The Lord is near to all who call on him,
to all who call on him in truth.

—Psalm 145:18

God of Suffering

In times of suffering, it's common to think that God has abandoned us, but the Bible gives us a completely different story. For some reason, God has chosen to be a sufferer, too. The prophet Hosea details his own suffering at the hands of an unfaithful wife, but it's clear that his woes are mirroring the suffering of God himself, whose

Seeking courage, Lord, I bundle my
fears and place them in your hands.
Too heavy for me, too weighty even to
ponder in this moment,
such shadowy terrors shrink
to size in my mind and—how
wonderful!—wither to nothing in
your grasp.

unfaithful people chase after false gods. "The more I called them, the more they went from me; they kept ... offering incense to idols," the Lord complains (Hosea 11:2).

Isaiah prophesies about a servant who will arise, but he would be "despised and rejected" and "a man of suffering" (Isaiah 53:3). The New Testament identifies Jesus as this servant. "By his wounds you have been healed," says Peter, quoting directly from Isaiah (1 Peter 2:24).

In that same passage, Peter speaks to slaves who suffered at the hands of unjust masters and Christians who suffered for their faith, suggesting that they were "called" to suffer like this—"because Christ also suffered for you, leaving you an example, so that you should follow in his steps" (v. 21).

Where is God when we are suffering emotionally from the loss of a loved one? He is suffering along with us. He is inviting us into his heart. Perhaps as we go through these difficult times, we'll understand more fully the feelings of our God.

> *Okay, Lord, the Footprints in the Sand thing. I used to laugh at that. Why, Lord, when it got bad, is there only one set of footprints? And you would answer: That, my child, is where I went off to get you some ice cream. Or something like that. It was just a cliché to me, until I started living it. I really did wonder why I felt so alone. Did you abandon me? Only now am I beginning to see how much you carried me through the hard times.*
>
> *I forgot to say it then, but now I say: Thank you.*

Mourning into Dancing

You have turned my mourning into dancing; you have taken off my sackcloth and clothed me with joy.

—Psalm 30:11

*I*t should have been a time of great celebration. Instead it was full of concern. Brian and Darlene were expecting their first child, but the delivery was difficult, and the child was in serious condition. The doctors managed to keep the baby alive for a few weeks. Those were agonizing weeks for the young parents, days and nights in the hospital, hoping against hope, yet fearing the worst.

They were not very religious people. They attended church occasionally, but they both had professional careers. Who had time? But now their lives had caved in as they watched the struggles of their newborn son, Jeremy. Prayers were flying heavenward, but would God really listen to a couple of part-time Christians?

Folks at their church got wind of the situation and rallied to support them. Suddenly people Brian and Darlene hardly knew were bringing them meals, sending them cards of encouragement, and offering to sit with them at the hospital. And, above all, they prayed for the young family.

How often we look upon God as our last and feeblest resource! We go to him because we have nowhere else to go. And then we learn that the storms of life have driven us, not upon the rocks, but into the desired haven.

—George MacDonald

Finally little Jeremy lost his struggle. His parents were devastated, but the church members stepped up their support. Over the next year, as Brian and Darlene worked through the grieving process, they were impressed by the caring nature of these Christians. The experience had shown these two affluent professionals how impoverished they were spiritually. They simply had no resources to get

He that lacks time to mourn,
lacks time to mend.
Eternity mourns that.
'Tis an ill cure for life's worst ills,
to have no time to feel them.
Where sorrow's held intrusive
and turned out,
There wisdom will not enter, nor true power,
Nor aught that dignifies humanity.
—Sir Henry Taylor

them through that crisis. Yet that was exactly what the church members had—and freely shared. The grieving parents, each in their own way, had a kind of conversion. The faith they had followed casually now became an important factor in their lives. They got involved in the church and began serving others, just as they had been served.

Looking back, they say it was their son Jeremy who brought them to Jesus.

Lord, let my sorrows become seeds, watered by my tears. Let the dirt and, well, manure of my environment provide nutrients for my growth. Let each downward turn of my experience be a root thrust into the nourishing soil. Let the scorching sun and slicing rain turn lush and green within me. Let the bracing winds teach this seedling to stand strong. Let me branch out through the seasons and bear fruit in due time.

Scars to Stars

You might not want to hear this right now, but it's true. Your greatest triumph may come from your worst calamity. Brian and Darlene are not alone. For many people, the tragedy of losing a loved one forces them to ask important questions—eternal questions. Coming so close to death makes us consider how precious life is. And what are we doing with that precious gift? Some find that bereavement propels them into action, as they try to make the most of whatever time they have left.

Trouble and anguish have come upon me, but your commandments are my delight . . . give me understanding that I may live.

—Psalm 119:143–144

We think that our pain is weakening us. We expect that our doubts will damage our faith. We assume that our future will be bleaker. But the truth is usually quite different. The crises we face tend to make us stronger. Through the pain and sorrow, we develop character, wisdom, and strength.

Healing is a matter of time,
But it is sometimes also a matter of opportunity.

— Hippocrates

In the Old Testament, God talks about "refining" his people like silver. "I have tested you in the furnace of adversity" (Isaiah 48:10). In the refining process, the impurities are burned out of metal, making the metal that much stronger.

My Redeemer,

I don't know how you're going to do it. I feel like such a wreck right now, like I have nothing to offer. This ordeal has sapped me. It has driven me down into the dirt and it has made me feel things I never want to feel again. But you want to turn all of that into something positive? I can't imagine what that would be, but I'm willing to let you try.

Take my life and let it be something beautiful for Thee.
Amen

The New Testament picks up on that idea in several places. "My brothers and sisters," writes James, "whenever you face trials of any kind, consider it nothing but joy, because you know that the testing of your faith produces endurance; and let endurance have its full effect, so that you may be mature and complete, lacking in nothing" (James 1:2–3). Paul talks about boasting in his sufferings, "knowing that suffering produces endurance, and endurance produces character, and character produces hope, and hope does not disappoint us, because God's love has been poured into our hearts" (Romans 5:3–5).

Then our mouth was filled with laughter, and our tongue with shouts of joy; then it was said among the nations, "The Lord has done great things for them."

—Psalm 126:2

You might feel that your grief will overwhelm you, that it will never go away. But, in fact, it is helping you grow. You will emerge from this a better person. As Psalm 30 tells us, the Lord can turn mourning into dancing. You can't ignore the sadness of losing your loved one, but you eventually grow into a celebration of that person's life—and your own.

And the one who was seated on the throne said, "See, I am making all things new.... To the thirsty I will give water as a gift from the spring of the water of life."

—Revelation 21:5–6

Using the Down Time

How can you use your time of grieving to grow stronger?
Consider these possibilities:

Experience God in a new way. Try being radically
honest with him about your feelings. Or try picturing
the Lord weeping beside you. Count on him for strength
as you deal with your grief each day. Brian and Darlene
were jolted into a fresh new relationship with God.
Maybe that can happen for you too.

*A new heart I will give you, and a new spirit I will
put within you; and I will remove from your body
the heart of stone and give you a heart of flesh.*
—Ezekiel 36:26

Exercise your emotions. Maybe you are already a very emotional person, but if you're not, this time of grieving can help you reconnect with your feelings. Our society today tends to discourage open displays of emotion. As a result many people bottle themselves up. Our strong reactions to the passing of a loved one can free us up to *feel* in ways that have long been dormant.

Going through a difficult time alone feels
like trying to find your way through
a pitch-black room. The moment you
reach out to another, a light appears that
guides you to the other side, where the
door to healing awaits.

Lord,
   You're asking me to dance?
You must not understand. I've
been in mourning. I've suffered
a great loss. You couldn't expect
me to—
   Turn mourning into dancing? I don't see how that's
possible. I haven't danced in so
long. There must be more
grieving to do.
   Please, not yet. I'm not
ready, am I? I've never been
very good on my feet, but now
you're leading me out onto the
dance floor. How can I resist?
   Lord, watch me dance. This
is for you.

Excavate your issues. This might be an opportunity to evaluate the way you relate to others. Consider your relationship with the loved one you've lost. It probably had some good aspects and some bad ones. You might harbor regrets or grudges. It might be healthy to get these out in the open. Proceed with care here, because your feelings might be pretty raw. You might want to work with a pastor or counselor on this, but if it's done well, it could teach you a lot about yourself as you move forward.

We know that all things work together for good for those who love God.

—Romans 8:28

Express compassion to others. In the future, when you meet anyone else who is grieving, you can say, "I've been there." You know what it's like, and that empowers you to sit beside others and offer help. It is an exhilarating feeling to "pay forward" the comfort you have received. When you use your negative experiences to enable you to comfort someone else, that's a powerful piece of redemption.

Faith in a wise and trustworthy God, even in grievous times like these, teaches us a new math: subtracting old ways and adding new thoughts because sharing with God divides our troubles and sadness and multiplies unfathomable possibilities for renewed life.

Every Remembrance

*I thank my God every time I remember you,
constantly praying with joy.*

—Philippians 1:3–4

They were a devout Christian family at the funeral of their 102-year-old matriarch. As they rode in the procession toward the cemetery, their conversation was upbeat. This was more of a beginning than an end. It was a graduation for this woman, who loved her Lord and looked forward to life in heaven. One family member after another commented on the joy of the occasion. She had lived a long, lovely life. This funeral was a celebration. Then the youngest granddaughter piped up. "Yeah, but I'm sad! I'm really going to miss her."

The positive approach of this family was perfectly legitimate. Everything they said was true. After more

114

than a century, it's hard to begrudge a saint's trip to heaven. But all their theologizing was covering up the simple emotional fact that death is also sad. It separates us from our loved ones. Even when we're happy for them, it's natural to miss them terribly. We can be glad *and* sad on the same occasion.

> *Lord, it's the little things that mean the most. The tilt of the head. The corner of a smile. The hand on my hand, telling me it will be all right. Inhaling a cup of coffee. Gazing with awe at a stunning sunset. Holding a squirming baby and rocking it to sleep. These are the things I remember, and I miss them all, but I treasure each one.*
>
> *Thank you for this life. Amen*

Heartwarming Surprise

As you deal with your own grief, you might find some uplift for your spirit by remembering the life of your departed loved one and thanking God for it. Sometimes funerals or memorial services provide opportunities for various people to comment on what the deceased meant to them. It can be a heartwarming surprise to see how many people were touched by the life of the departed.

Pleasant but quiet, Gus worked for many years in the mailroom of a Christian ministry. The executives at

> *My friend lives on in me,*
> *in thought and memory,*
> *remembrance of the time we*
> *spent together.*
> *And though my friend is gone*
> *our relationship goes on,*
> *for I know that friendship*
> *lasts forever.*

I see a robin's egg hatching, Lord, and am set free from my doubts and fretting. For, while life is not always filled with joy and happiness, I know it is always held in your hand.

It's a pleasure to share one's memories. Everything remembered is dear, endearing, touching, precious. At least the past is safe—though we didn't know it at the time. We know it now. Because it's in the past; because we have survived.

—Susan Sontag

that company viewed him as sort of a lovable loser. He wasn't very well-educated, had few social skills, and suffered from an assortment of health problems—but he managed to do his job faithfully.

Remember the days of old,
consider the years long past.
—Deuteronomy 32:7

Gus passed away in his mid-40s, an untimely death, but not surprising, given his health history. Some of the staff of the ministry where he worked went to the funeral at a nearby church. *That* was surprising. Since Gus was single and lived by himself, they expected only a smattering of relatives and friends, but the place was packed. Over the course of the next two hours, one person after another stood up and told of the kindness Gus had shown them.

He taught me to read. He drove me to church each Sunday. He helped me quit drinking. He got me a job. The staff members were shocked; they had no idea what a great guy they'd been working with.

These public remembrances help us celebrate the life of someone we've lost. They give us perspective on the person's life. They provide us with a sense of thankfulness that can soften our grief. They also help us to say goodbye.

Of course we can find private ways to remember our departed loved ones as well. We can place pictures of them and various artifacts from their lives around our homes. Or you might choose to create photo albums or scrapbooks to commemorate the person's life. Perhaps you could even put together a video or audio recording of various people's memories of your loved one. Some activity-oriented folks might do something special in their loved one's honor—plant a tree, walk in the woods, skip stones on the river, walk barefoot in the rain, climb a mountain, ride a train, or do some other particular thing the departed loved. In those cases, it's almost as if the lost loved one is enjoying the activity too.

> *Dear God,*
>
> *I'm going to start singing again. My voice has been quiet too long. Not that I'm "getting over" my grief. No, I doubt I'll ever recover entirely from the loss of this special person in my life. How can I? But I can sing again because this special person would want me to. Because they are so special, I can celebrate every memory. I can live my life fully, as a way of thumbing my nose at death.*
>
> *Celebrate with me, dear Lord.*
>
> *Amen*

The Trouble with Remembrance

But some have trouble with such remembrance. The grief might be too fresh. Especially in the early months of bereavement, being surrounded by reminders of the person might create unbearable sadness. Be sensitive to your own needs (and the needs of anyone else in your home). There are times when you want to remember and times when you don't.

What happens when the person you're commemorating wasn't such a saint? How can you memorialize someone you blame for messing up your life in one way or another? Do you grit your teeth and pretend they were perfect?

This is a problem for many who grieve the loss of their parents. They truly love and miss their folks, but there are all sorts of issues too. Can you forgive someone after they're gone? Or should you just forget all the bad stuff?

121

Honesty is the best policy, but grace makes it even better. When we live in grace, we understand that we are sinners forgiven by God, and other people are too. We don't need to ignore the bad things done by those we've lost, but we shouldn't dwell on those things either. In cases where we've been wronged, we can offer forgiveness belatedly. Why not assume that the person is straightening things out with the Lord right now and would be asking your forgiveness if that were possible? Would you grant that forgiveness?

In other cases, we find our memories haunted by our own sense of guilt and regret. We feel bad about things we did to the person who is now gone. For some reason, we never got around to seeking forgiveness, and now that's impossible.

Or is it? That's a transaction you can bring before the Lord. Confess your sins and ask for God's forgiveness for whatever you did or didn't do with regard to your departed loved one. Ask him to clear the guilt from your memory.

Then you need to show grace to yourself. You're not perfect; that's a given. You could have done more, said more, loved more. Maybe your relationship with this person was not all it could have been. But you can still be thankful for what it was.

> *My God,*
>
> *Thank you for the life of the loved one I've lost. Yes, I've been grieving over the loss, and even scolding you a bit, but now I'm looking from a different angle. This dear one meant so much to me. You ministered to me through this person, and I am grateful for that. So instead of regretting the moments we'll no longer have together, I will savor the moments we had. Thank you.*
>
> *Amen*

"I thank my God every time I remember you," the apostle Paul said in nearly every epistle (see Ephesians 1:16; Philippians 1:3; 1 Thessalonians 1:2). And what kind of memories did he have? Oh, he'd been arrested in some of these towns, beaten up, and jailed. In some of these churches, rival preachers came along with their trash talk, saying that Paul's teaching was bogus and that they had a better way. Some of these congregations had bitter infighting. They weren't perfect people, but Paul thanked God for them anyway.

And *that's* the attitude we can adopt toward the loved one we've lost—thankful remembrance—even though they weren't perfect and neither are we.

A Memory Prayer

Rewound and shown over again, like old home movies,
tales are being told, O Lord, by those of us facing this loss.
"Remember when?" we say laughing, interrupting one
another in the retelling of time shared.
"Remember when?" We savor a final showing, reel upon
reel, of pranks pulled, triumphs achieved, kindnesses
shown, conversations held. "Remember when?"
We are grateful that you bring a last frame into focus for
us, of life forever after, of rooms prepared for us. And while
we shrink against daily life without this loved one, we're
comforted knowing they've just gone on ahead.
Thank you, Lord, for adding the gift of memory to our
days ahead, of helping us to "remember when."
Polish our memories of loved ones laid to rest here, Lord,
and then strengthen our resolve for going on without them.

Comfort My People

Comfort, O comfort my people, says your God.

—Isaiah 40:1

*Y*ou're not alone. There are other relatives and friends who have been hurt by the loss of this loved one. Many of them are going through the same process you are. That's why we have funerals—to bring together the grieving community, to share our sorrow.

And there is a wider community around you, a group of believers who want to help you through the crisis. They're not always sure what to say or do, but they're concerned about you. They want to encourage you, empower you, and salve your wounds.

Ironically, grief can be a very private thing. Many people prefer to withdraw from the crowds when they're hurting.

They feel emotionally out of control, and they don't want to embarrass themselves in front of others. Some feel a need to put on a strong face, to seem "together" in this crisis, so that people whisper that they're "taking things remarkably well." But at a certain point, they just wish everybody would go away, so they can sort through their feelings on their own.

Maybe that's your story; maybe not. There are some people who prefer to grieve in the company of caring friends. But for the most part, mourning is an activity that's both private and public. The question is: *How do you deal with the people who comfort you?*

Therefore encourage one another and build up each other, as indeed you are doing.

—1 Thessalonians 5:11

Listen to their heart. People may say some stupid things. Their words may be sappy or silly or inappropriate or mildly offensive, but they're just trying to help. Think about the times in the past when you've been in their shoes, searching for something to say to comfort someone. It's not easy. We send pastors to seminary to learn stuff like that. The rest of us mutter reassurances like, "It's all for the best"; "He's probably happier now"; or "You'll forget all about her."

Through companionship, Gracious God, that you send to travel alongside me, I feel myself warmed, uplifted and inspired by friends, family and those who've traveled the same road.

—Miguel de Unamuno

The words really aren't important, are they? They're rather irrelevant. If you videotaped these encounters and turned off the sound, you'd get the essential elements: the loving look, the supportive hand. These people want to say the right thing; they just don't know what that is. Don't hold that against them. Receive the warm wishes of their heart, no matter what the words.

The thread of our life would be dark, heaven knows,
if it were not with friendship and love intertwined.
—Sir Thomas Moore, *Friendship Is a Special Gift*

You can comfort them, but you don't have to. Some mourning family members feel a need to comfort others who come to the funeral or call on them in the days that follow. It's just in their nature. They want everyone to feel good, and this sad occasion puts pressure on them

Lord,
Thank you for all
the precious people who
have stood by me in my
time of need. When I was
in the pit of depression,
they sat there with me.
When I was too weepy to
eat, they fed me. When
I needed to cry out in
grief and anger, they
gave me pillows to punch
and dishes to throw. And
when I needed to remem-
ber, they brought out the
photo album. Their gifts
have sustained me in my
darkest hour, and I thank
you, Lord, for working
through them.
Amen

to provide comfort. As a result, there's extra stress piled upon the sorrow. They don't feel free to express their own grief, because that might drag others down.

If that's your tendency, don't get caught in that trap. Remember, you have your own grief to work through. It's not your responsibility to lift the spirits of others. They are there to help you. And what you need, more than anything, is to feel your true feelings. You aren't hurting anyone else by expressing your emotions. That's why your comforters are there—to help you do just that.

Father God, thank you for my many friends who stand beside me in all situations. They are always there when I need them to listen, laugh, and cry.

131

Let the tears flow. Some people will do anything to avoid crying in public. It's not "manly." It makes your makeup run. It seems childish. The dearly departed "wouldn't have wanted" that. People have all sorts of reasons, but none of them "hold water," so to speak. This is your time to grieve. You're allowed to cry. You're *supposed* to cry. People expect it. So open the floodgates in your heart and let your emotion flow. No need to run to the restroom to sob in private. Just have plenty of tissues available.

Bear one another's burdens, and
in this way you will fulfil
the law of Christ.

—Galatians 6:2

Tears are a cleansing agent. This is true physically as well as emotionally. God has wired us to cry in times of distress, and this qualifies. It's healthy to weep and unhealthy to hold back.

Find your private times. People come, sometimes from far away, to share your grief. You need to spend time with them, to let them do that. But you also need some personal time and other time alone with just the closest mourners. When the crowds are too much to take, it's okay to withdraw for a while. People will understand.

Two are better than one . . .
if they fall, one will lift up the other.

—Ecclesiastes 4:9–10

Psychologists talk about introverts and extroverts. This distinction has little to do with how much of a show-off you are; it's about where you get your energy. Introverts gain energy when they're alone and expend it in public. After being with people for too long, they need to go off by themselves and recharge. Extroverts draw energy from others and find it taxing to be alone. You may find this applicable to your grieving process. If you're an extrovert, you may need a group of caring friends who can work through your grief with you. If you're an introvert, you will need many private moments along the way to refuel.

Weep with those who weep.

—Romans 12:15

Lord, save me from my comforters. I know they mean well, but sometimes they say the silliest things. If one more person tells me to "cheer up," I think I'll slug them. (Lord, give me patience, now!) It's hard enough careening through every emotion you created without having these "friends" directing traffic.

All right, Lord. I know I need to receive their gifts of love and be grateful, but it's hard sometimes. Help me to have patience.

Amen

Tell them what you need. In this mourning period, you are the center of attention. That might feel uncomfortable for you, especially if you're used to caring for everyone else, but that's the way it is. People are there to care for you—so let them. But they might need some coaching.

We have a Christian duty
to encourage one another.
Many a time a word of
praise or thanks or
appreciation or cheer
has kept a man on his feet.
Blessed is the man
who speaks such a word.

—William Barclay, *The Gospel of Matthew*

As mentioned earlier, people with caring hearts don't always say the right thing. They don't always do the right thing either. You may need to tell them how to care for you. What do you need? This starts with the funeral arrangements and proceeds through the grieving process. You can't expect people to read your mind. Ask them to sing a song, help with your taxes, babysit your kids, or call you every Friday.

You might feel selfish about that, but you're actually just helping the process work. The task is to provide comfort for you. You need to be the foreperson of your crew, telling people how to accomplish this. In most cases, they will be grateful for the direction.

Therefore encourage one another with these words.

—1 Thessalonians 4:18

*Sometimes I want to be
alone.*
  *But thank God
you're there, my friend.*
*Sometimes I need a
good cry.*
  *But you have a way
of making me laugh.*
*Sometimes I feel as if
God has given up on
me.*
  *But I sense his
presence in you.*
*Sometimes I can't sleep
from grief.*
  *And you wait up
with me.*
*Sometimes I want to be
alone.*
  *But I know you are
there for me.*
  Thank God.

Grab some comforters for the long-term. There's a funnel effect with bereavement. The time of the funeral is usually a whirlwind of activity, with all sorts of people, some you hardly know, rushing around to help you. In the following week or so, you get some cards and flowers. And then ... it's a wasteland.

That might be overstating it slightly, but the truth is that you might need a listening ear two months after your

The people God surrounds us with
are making a difference in our
lives and write indelible lines on
hearts, souls, and minds. We read
between them God's message of
grace and celebrate how
far we've come.

loss. You might need a night out six months down the road. You might need a note of encouragement next time your birthday or anniversary rolls around. By then, most of the comforters will have forgotten about you.

God promises us his comfort, but he also uses us as his agents to comfort others. In fact, the difficulties we've gone through often give us the ability to reassure others who are now going through the same experiences. How will God use you to extend comfort to someone else?

But not all of them. You can help yourself by assembling a small corps of caring friends. Look around for the people who seem especially interested in helping, those who say, "Let me know if there's anything I can do," and really mean it. Take them up on that offer. Ask them to check up on you throughout the next year or two. If they're truly gifted in caring, they'll understand, and they'll appreciate the request. (If you can't identify such comforters yourself, you might ask your pastor to suggest some people from the congregation.)

Too often we lie
when people say,
How are you?
We say, "I'm fine."
We smile, and put
on our happy face.

Why can't we be honest,
at least with loved ones,
and say, "I hurt"?
Why can't we cry honest tears
and let a friend
comfort us for a moment—
embrace us
with loving arms,
as we take off
the mask we wear
to hide the pain?

As you emerge, look for others to comfort. It might seem like a distant hope at this point, but you will emerge from the grieving process with renewed spirits and restored health. And you will have gained something extremely important—an empathy for others who have suffered loss. You will have learned about comforting from the vantage point of the one who receives comfort. That's a valuable piece of education that will equip you to provide effective comfort to others.

So pay attention as you continue on the road to health. Take notes. Someday you can use your pain for the gain of others.

> *Lord, dismiss us with thy blessing,*
> *Hope, and comfort from above;*
> *Let us each, thy peace possessing,*
> *Triumph in redeeming love.*
> —Robert Hawker, "Benediction"

*We can give touch and comfort and
strength in physical healing, but for
spiritual healing we need to turn to
God. So, knowing our strengths and
our weaknesses, we turn to the Lord
because all of us carry our past hurts,
and He has the remedy for everything.
It's simple: If we just turn to Him, He
will bring us this inner healing, this
spiritual healing so we can make our
lives more holy and more pleasing to
God.*

—Sister Dolores, quoted by Mother Teresa of Calcutta,
A Simple Path

Fear No Evil

Though I walk through the darkest valley,
I fear no evil; for you are with me.

—Psalm 23:4

When Nancy's husband was diagnosed with amyotrophic lateral sclerosis, also known as Lou Gehrig's disease, she was completely devastated.

You will not fear the terror of the night,
or the arrow that flies by day,
or the pestilence that stalks
in darkness, or the destruction
that wastes at noonday.

—Psalm 91:5–6

Once a robust man, he was gradually debilitated by
the disease. The stages of Nancy's grief actually began
during this time. At first, she was numb, in shock.
Her huband kept working as a carpenter, and neither
of them wanted to admit what was ahead. But before
long he couldn't grasp a hammer, and then he needed a
wheelchair.

Though we stumble, we shall not fall headlong,
for the Lord holds us by the hand.

—Psalm 37:24

There were times of anger—at the disease, at the doctors,
at God—and time spent grasping at miracle cures. Then
finally, two years after the diagnosis, he was gone, and
Nancy plunged into the process again. But after another
year, she seemed to have regained a certain equilibrium.
Except for those occasional reminders. "Our anniversary

was a hard time," says Nancy. "Sometimes just seeing his chair in the living room would make me cry. Or I would slip back after hearing a song that was ours."

*When I thought, "My foot is slipping,"
your steadfast love, O Lord, held me up.
When the cares of my heart are many,
your consolations cheer my soul.*

—Psalm 94:18–19

Experts call it "the slippery slope." Just when you think you've licked one stage and moved on to the next, you slip back. And even after you've "recovered," you will probably be surprised and dismayed by some backward lapses. *Where did that come from? Do I have to go through all of that again?*

Almighty God,
Protect me from
my own crazy emotions.
These days I don't know
whether I'm coming or
going. I'm angry, de-
pressed, and oddly opti-
mistic, all in the same day.
I'm confusing my friends
and terrifying myself. It's
like I have no control over
how I feel. And just when I
think I'm moving on, get-
ting over it, ready to start
my life anew—wham!—I
get blindsided by some
new emotion. Am I going
crazy? I don't think so, but
it sure feels that way.
Lord, save me from
all this. You're the only
one who can.
Amen

No, you don't. For years after your loss, you can expect to flashback momentarily to stages you thought you were finished with. It doesn't mean you're crazy. It means you're normal.

Of course, these flashes of sadness or anger or temptation can still be quite frightening. Some will arrive on cue: birthdays, anniversaries, holidays. Some will be triggered by places you've visited together in the past. Even a movie, a TV show, or (as in Nancy's case) a song can bring back those feelings. Maybe it's the clothes you're wearing that your loved one bought for you.

Every tomorrow has two handles.
We can take hold of it with the handle
of anxiety or the handle of faith.

—Henry Ward Beecher

So do not worry about tomorrow,
for tomorrow will bring more
worries of its own.
Today's trouble is
enough for today.

—Matthew 6:34

In all these cases, the memories trigger something else, some unfinished business. For a moment, perhaps, you need to go back into denial and pretend that your loved one is still nearby. Or maybe you focus on some regret or some issue you never resolved with that person.

A widow might be going through her finances a year after her husband's death and suddenly blurt out in anger, "Why didn't you keep records of these investments?" She might be stunned by her own vehemence, but it's not

Lord of Life,
 I declare it here and now: I am mad at death. I feel that death cheated me out of a good relationship, and now it seems the powers of death are doing a number on my soul. I feel dragged down. I feel as if a huge part of me has died. And now, as I look around, I see death everywhere—in war, in crime, in immorality, in apathy. The whole world seems to be dead and dying, and that really bothers me. What can we do about it?
 I humbly ask you to raise me to new life.
 Amen

really about record-keeping. It's about the anger that's still buried within her. She really means to say, "Why did you die? I'm still hurting because you left." It's good to get those feelings out. Chances are, she's not plunging back into a three-month anger jag. It's just a droplet left in the pipeline. It needed to trickle out.

Finish each day and be done with it. Tomorrow is a new day, you shall begin it serenely.

—Ralph Waldo Emerson

On the third anniversary of a child's death, a man might go to a bar and get drunk. It's a quick-fix strategy, a way to escape the pain, but it's something he stopped doing years ago. Why this relapse? After all this time, he thought the pain was behind him. But now, it is as fresh as if the death just happened. Apparently his painful memories caught him at a weak moment. Chances are, he'll realize that this bender doesn't really fix anything. He'll pick himself up, dust himself off, and continue forward.

In Psalm 23, we read about walking through "the darkest valley." In a way, that's the bereavement process—a

It is you who light my lamp;
the Lord, my God, lights
up my darkness.

—Psalm 18:28

long walk through a dark valley. And it is the shadow of death—the death of our loved one—that looms over us, blocking the light, keeping us from seeing a clear path.

*Give us grace and strength
to forbear and to persevere.
Give us courage and gaiety
and the quiet mind . . . give us
the strength to encounter that
which is to come, that we may
be brave in peril, constant in
tribulation, temperate in wrath,
and in all changes of fortune,
and, down to the gates of
death, loyal and loving to one
another.*

—Robert Louis Stevenson

At various points along the way—Denial Bluff, Anger Canyon, the Quick-Fix Quicksand, or the Pit of Depression—the terrain is difficult. We fear we might get stuck. And even when we think we're free and clear, we find ourselves under that shadow again from time to time. It's just part of the process.

"I will fear no evil," the psalmist says, "for you are with me" (23 v. 4). The Lord is shepherding us through that recovery process. Step by step, and even through our relapses, he will keep moving us forward. He gives us the courage to keep putting one foot in front of the other.

In the dark sea of my despair, dear God, I am afraid, lost, and alone. But I will not give up hope. I will cast out my heart one more time into the deep waters and await your loving salvation.

Rock of my Salvation,
*   Free me from fear.*
Give me the courage I need
to get through each day.
My heart feels raw, as if it
could burst at any moment.
But I don't want to go
through life on eggshells. I
want to live boldly. I want
to dance. But fear holds me
back.
*   Keep whispering your*
comfort in my ear. Keep
letting me know you are
right there beside me. Keep
leading me down the path
you have set for me.
*   Amen*

A Future with Hope

For surely I know the plans I have for you,
says the Lord, plans for your welfare and
not for harm, to give you a future with hope.

—Jeremiah 29:11

J eremiah is known as "the weeping prophet,"
and with good reason. He had bad news for the
nation of Judah. They would be conquered by an enemy
country, and many of their citizens would be taken
captive. He predicted 70 years of captivity.

I am confident of this, that the one who began
a good work among you will bring it to
completion by the day of Jesus Christ.

—Philippians 1:6

156

Of course, the people didn't want to hear it, so Jeremiah proclaimed his prophecy louder and stronger. The nation was in for a bad time ahead. They could try to deny that fact, but it would happen nonetheless.

Hope is that thing with feathers
that perches in the soul and
sings the tune without
the words and never
stops . . . at all.

——Emily Dickinson

Yet this prophet's message was not all gloom and doom. The time of captivity would eventually end, and God would restore his people. In the Scripture that leads off this chapter, the Lord discusses his "plans." He would give them a "future with hope."

There's a slight similarity between Jeremiah's message and the message of this book. No, I'm not claiming that this is Holy Writ, but I am predicting that you may face some bad times over the next year or two. As you work through the grief of losing a loved one, things will get worse before they get better.

But they will get better.

Grant, O Lord, to all who are bereaved the spirit of faith and courage, that they may have the strength to meet the days to come with steadfastness and patience; not sorrowing as those without hope, but in thankful remembrance of your great goodness, and in the joyful expectation of eternal life with those they love.

—*Book of Common Prayer*, Church of England

Lord of yesterday, today, and tomorrow,

I now see that you've been with me all along. Even in those challenging times, you were holding me tight.

I understand that you're with me right now. When I need a word to say, you supply it. When I need comfort, you soothe my soul.

And now I need to trust you with my future. Where is all of this going? What's ahead for me? Only you can know that.

I don't know what the future holds, but I know you hold the future.

Amen

It might be the furthest thing from your mind right now, but you will be happy again. That doesn't mean you'll forget about the one you've lost—far from it. You will treasure their memory, thankful for the time you had together. But your life will go on. You will try some new things. You will develop other relationships. You will discover new strength of character. You will find surprising new ways to help other people. And you will have a more resilient relationship with God.

Listen to what the Lord said through Jeremiah: "I will fulfil to you my promise and bring you back to

Hope. Heaven's own gift to struggling mortals;
pervading, like some subtle essence from the skies, all
things, both good and bad; as universal as death,
and more infectious than disease!
—Charles Dickens, *Nicholas Nickleby*

this place. For surely I know the plans I have for you, says the Lord, plans for your welfare and not for harm, to give you a future with hope. Then when you call upon me and come and pray to me, I will hear you. When you search for me, you will find me; if you seek me with all your heart, I will let you find me, says the Lord, and I will restore your fortunes" (Jeremiah 29:10–14).

It's clear that the Lord wants to be close to you. He knows what you're going through. He understands that your relationship with him might be a bit rocky right now. But it won't always be that way. He will help you sort through your expectations and assumptions about him, and he'll work with you to build a new way of interacting, based on the reality of who he is. Despite your questions and doubts—no, actually *because of* your questions and doubts—the Lord will be a powerful force in your life.

*A future with hope. That's what I
        long for.*
*. Tomorrows that teem with
        adventure.*
After my desolate winter of grief
Hope springs eternal for me.

*You've guided me through the long
        pathway of healing,*
*Salved me and saved me and
        satisfied longings.*
Now I see visions of glory ahead,
A future of purpose and joy.

Lead me on, my King, my Healer.
Unfold the life that remains.
*Let my existence bring praise to
        you always.*
*May others grow strong through
        my pain.*

Living with Hope

In the throes of depression, you get nearsighted. That is, you start looking only at this day, this room, this problem. You're not thinking about the wider world. You have little sense of the future. You just want to get through the day. If you're functioning at all, you are plodding rather than walking—certainly not dancing.

Hope is about believing with a humble heart that tomorrow can be different. It's about knowing that light will come to chase away this darkness.

As the depression lifts, your sight changes. No, not the strength of your glasses, but the way you see your life. You begin to look at larger issues. You begin to think about your future. You even begin to hope.

In fact, *hope* might be the key word for that change. Hopelessness turns to hopefulness. For the first time in a year or so, things are looking up.

With hope, then, comes the *courage* to step out of your protective shell. Maybe you learn to love again (not necessarily in a romantic way, but at least in the form of a solid new friendship). Maybe you start thinking again about your goals in life. You've just come face-to-face with death; what do you want to accomplish in the time you have left? Maybe there's some new ministry you want to launch or join. Can you pass on your wisdom to a new generation by teaching Sunday school? Can you reach out to less fortunate folks by working in a soup

O Christ, Son of the living God,
may Your holy angels guard our
sleep,
may they watch us as we rest
And hover around our beds.
Let them reveal to us in our
dreams
visions of your glorious truth,
O High Prince of the universe,
O High Priest of the mysteries.
May no dreams disturb our rest
and no nightmares darken our
dreams.
May no fears or worries delay
our willing, prompt repose.
May the virtue of our daily work
hallow our nightly prayers.
May our sleep be deep and soft
So our work be fresh and hard.

—St. Patrick

kitchen? Can you raise money for research to fight the disease that took your loved one?

Hope allows you to look forward rather than backward. Instead of mourning what you've lost from the past, you use your past experiences to propel you into the future. And, having gone through grief, you have battle-tested your emotions. You can take some new chances because you're not as brittle as you used to be.

He will wipe every tear from their eyes.
Death will be no more; mourning and
crying and pain will be no more,
for the first things have passed away.

——Revelation 21:4

God's Great Faithfulness

Are you there yet? Are you ready to move forward in hope? Maybe not. You might still be working through the process. If that's the case, dog-ear these pages and come back to them later. Hope will be there for you when you're ready. And maybe just knowing that will help you get through some difficult days.

Jeremiah did that sort of thing. He knew all about the hopeful future God had promised, but it was still tough to see his nation ravished. The Book of Lamentations records his reaction to the destruction of Jerusalem, something he had warned about, but people didn't want to hear his message.

"He has filled me with bitterness. He has sated me with wormwood. He has made my teeth grind on gravel, and made me cower in ashes; my soul is bereft of peace; I have forgotten what happiness is; so I say, 'Gone is

my glory, and all that I had hoped for from the Lord.' "
(Lamentations 3:15–18).

Maybe you've been there. Happiness is a distant
memory. Jeremiah describes his feelings in bitter terms.
His soul is "bowed down" within him.

Then he turns a corner. "But this I call to mind, and
therefore I have hope: The steadfast love of the Lord
never ceases, his mercies never come to an end; they
are new every morning; great is your faithfulness"
(vs. 21–23).

For several pages he has been describing the destruction
of his city. Buildings toppled. People hurting, homeless.
Still he hails the steadfast love of the Lord. God's
mercies are brand new day after day after day.

He goes on to declare that the Lord is his "portion." God
is enough. "Therefore I will hope in him" (v. 24).

There's that word again. *Hope*. Grab it. Shelve it for the future, maybe, but don't forget about it. Claim it. Use it. Let it propel you into a glorious future.

> *Loving Lord,*
> *I pulled open the shade this morning and the sunshine burst into my room. It seemed to burst into my life. I've been wearing blinders for months now, closing my eyes to the radiant existence you're offering. But now I think I'm ready. Lead me forward into the life you want for me. Give me the wisdom I need, the courage I need, the character I need to honor you as I take these next steps.*
> *I trust you for all this.*
> *Amen*

Reflections

*Blessed be the God and Father of our Lord Jesus Christ,
the Father of mercies and the God of all consolation,
who consoles us in all our affliction.*

2 Corinthians 1:3–4

*H*ealing takes time. And just when you feel you've turned a corner, you might suddenly find yourself cast down again. There may be times when you need a little extra comfort to make it through the day. When that happens, you can turn to this selection of prayers and quotes and take a quiet moment to reflect and pray. May these words bring you some measure of peace in this difficult time.

Steer the ship of my life, good Lord, to your quiet harbour, where I can be safe from the storms of sin and conflict. Show me the course I should take. Renew in me the gift of discernment, so that I can always see the right direction in which I should go. And give me the strength and courage to choose the right course, even when the sea is rough and the waves are high, knowing that through enduring hardship and danger in your name we shall find comfort and peace.

——Basil of Caesarea

There is a sanctuary of peace within us that we can access anytime by doing a simple breathing meditation. We close our eyes and focus on our breath as it goes in and out of our body. We clear the mind of all turmoil, gently keeping our focus on the breath. In time, thoughts fade, and we begin to feel a sense of connectedness with a higher presence. We keep breathing, gently, quietly, and we touch the face of God.

How sweet the silent backward tracings! The wanderings as in dreams—the meditation of old times resumed—their loves, joys, persons, voyages.

—Walt Whitman, "Memories"

Our journey together does not end when one person dies. We continue to walk the same path, only now one of us walks on solid ground, and the other floats alongside in the realm of pure spirit.

To receive the blessings of healing, the heart must be open. When we are grieving, it is so easy to close off the heart as if a prison and throw away the key, sure that we will never be able to love again. But a heart that is shut down cannot receive understanding, acceptance, and renewal. Even though we feel angry and afraid, we must keep the heart's door slightly ajar so that God's grace can enter and fill our darkness with the light of hope.

If time is the great physician, then love is the caring aide who works side by side, hand in hand with time to heal our pain and bring us back to the living.

Sometimes our fears and doubts about the goodness of life are overshadowed by what is happening to us and around us. The death of a loved one is one of these times. But we are told to have faith, to look beyond the surface of things, and allow the possibility of miracles to exist. Grief shuts us down emotionally for a while, but if we keep a part of us open and receptive to life, we may find the blessing after all.

Our Comforting Lord

Lord Jesus,
You are medicine to me when I am sick,
Strength to me when I need help,
Life itself when I fear death,
The way when I long for heaven,
The light when all is dark,
And food when I need nourishment.
Glory be to you forever.
Amen.

—Saint Ambrose

God, Your love moves mountains; please now move a mountain of grief from my path. Your grace creates miracles; please send me a miracle of newfound joy in a life that right now holds no happiness. Your power heals the sick at heart; please comfort me with a soothing balm that calms and nourishes my dried-up soul. God, pour yourself upon me like the rain that brings new life to a dry Earth.
Amen

As one season changes, a new season unfolds, bringing with it new gifts. Life and death are part of a natural cycle of closings and openings, endings and beginnings.

Dear Lord,
In my hour of grief, be the guiding light
that directs me through my pain.
In my day of despair, be the gentle hand
that leads me out of the dark woods.
In my moment of need, be the tower I
lean upon for strength and assurance.
In the night of my anguish, be the
presence that comforts and soothes me
like a mother to a child.
In the time of my suffering, Dear Lord,
be my friend and constant companion.
For this I am grateful.
Amen

We ask over and over again "Why?" but the answer does not come readily. Only with time and healing can we begin to understand and to know that a grand design is at work in our lives, and that the grand designer has not abandoned us or forsaken us at all.

God, give me rest from the labor of my suffering. Give me comfort from the work of my mind and heart to understand why this has happened. Give me healing from the pain that wracks my body and the grief that has a stranglehold upon my heart. I turn to you, dear God, to soothe me with your grace and love, that I may be able to lift myself up from the depths of my sorrow and face the rest of my life with a renewed sense of purpose amidst my personal loss.

Where before my heart was like a desert, desolate and empty of life because of my deep despair, God has set the rain of his loving grace upon me and I am now beginning to bloom again. Where before my soul was a wasteland, with no life in it because of my suffering over this terrible loss, God has tilled new ground and set the foundation for a great and mighty fortress of healing to rise upon once-spoiled lands. I am a garden overflowing with new, lush life, and I owe it all to the grace and love of God.

Blessings, like miracles, appear only when we believe in them. Faith gives us the eyes with which to see and the ability to believe what we are seeing.

*Grief comes in seasons. The cold,
numbness of autumn blows through
the soul as we grope to accept what
has happened. The fall gives way
to the dark despair of winter where
the sun refuses to shine. But then we
witness the first glimmer of spring, and
our hearts begin to feel a little lighter.
Hope spreads like sunshine and we
bloom under its warmth, where before
we were withered and deadened. We
breathe again, and fresh air fills our
hungry lungs. We bask in the glow of
summer, grateful to be alive.*

There's a story about a father and daughter working in the garden. The little girl aims the hose to water the thirsty plants, only to find that the flow is suddenly cut off. She cries, "Daddy, what happened?" He smiles, pointing out the problem. Her foot had stepped upon the hose, cutting off the flow. Once she removes her foot, the abundant flow returns. Our relationship with God is like this. It is always within our power to keep the flow of God's love open and abundant in times of need.

I swear I think there is nothing but immortality!
That the exquisite scheme is for it, and the nebulous
float is for it, and the cohering is for it!
And all the preparation is for it—and identity is for
it—and life and materials are altogether for it!

——Walt Whitman

Love is a gift we give. Love is a gift we receive from
others. Even those who are gone continue to give and
receive love. Love knows no fences, no restraints, and
no confinements.

Lord in Heaven, work a miracle in our hardened hearts and shine the light of your love upon our gloomy corners, where we now cower in our fear and pain. Bring us this day our daily bread, our daily hope, and our daily strength, and then bring it to us all over again tomorrow. Lord, with your help we can overcome any difficulty, rise above any challenge, face any fear, and cope with any loss. Shower down upon us your healing love like manna for the hungry in heart and soul.

It is not just the storm cloud that brings us the opportunity for growth and understanding, but the hopeful expectancy of the rainbow behind it.

Father, Mother, God. You who have made the moon and the stars and the sun. You who have given life its own rhythm and pattern. You who have instilled a divine order and timing to everything under the heavens. Make me resilient like the sandy beach upon which the waves crash. Make me strong like the mighty willow tree that bends but does not break in the high winds. Give me the patience and wisdom to know that my suffering will one day turn to a greater understanding of your ways, your works, and your wonders.

Visiting beside still, tranquil waters,
I find peace. Like a shell, I carry it
home to hold against my ear and be
soothed again by its repeated
message and am again restored
even on my arid daily shore.

The circle of life remains unbroken by the experience
of death. Like a wheel forever turning, the sun
continues to rise and set, the tides continue to swell
and withdraw from the shore, and that which has
died continues to move along the wheel, even though
our eyes cannot discern it.

The glory of God is evident in all of his vast creation. The glory of God is in love, music, good food, and laughter. But the glory of God is also in pain and suffering; when people are called upon to be more of themselves and to help one another cope. It is in the darkest times that humankind becomes more like God: stronger, resilient, full of faith. It is easy to see God's glory in good things. The truly wise person sees the glory of God even in the bad.

*I know, dear God, that this too shall pass. Even as
I am in the midst of this pain and despair, I can see
the light at the end of the long, dark tunnel. I can see
the light of your love for me and the wisdom these
trials will give me. I can see the brighter day ahead,
filled with laughter and joy and new beginnings.
Knowing this, I carry on toward the light.*

*Time and space cannot separate those who love.
For love transcends all limitations, rises above all
boundaries. Love knows only the realm of the
unlimited.*

In Times of...

*T*he Bible has words to inspire, comfort, and guide you. This index will help you know what Bible verses to turn to in times of need or crisis.

Anger
Psalm 4:4
Psalm 37:8
Proverbs 14:17
Proverbs 15:1
Proverbs 22:24–25
Proverbs 27:4
Ecclesiastes 7:9
Matthew 5:22
Ephesians 4:26, 31–32
1 Timothy 2:8

Death
Psalm 33:18–19
John 3:16
Romans 6:23
1 Corinthians 15:51–52
2 Corinthians 5:1–4
Philippians 1:20–24
Hebrews 2:14–15
Revelation 2:11

Depression
Job 3
Psalm 6:8–10
Psalm 30:10–12
Psalm 31:12–14
Psalm 42:9–11
Psalm 56:8–11
Psalm 94:17–19
Proverbs 14:13–14
Ecclesiastes 7:3–5
2 Corinthians 1:3–5

Discouragement
Joshua 1:6–9
Esther 4:13–16
Isaiah 1:17
Romans 1:11–12
Colossians 2:1–3
1 Thessalonians 5:11–14
Hebrews 3:13
Hebrews 10:25

Fear
Psalm 23:4
Psalm 27:1
Isaiah 41:10
Luke 12:4–5
Philippians 2:12
2 Timothy 1:7

Illness
Psalm 41:4
Psalm 107:19–20
Psalm 147:3
Isaiah 53:5
Isaiah 58:8
Jeremiah 33:6
Malachi 4:2
Matthew 8:16–17
John 4:46–53
1 Corinthians 12:9
James 5:14–15

Indecision
Psalm 27:13
Isaiah 33:6
Romans 8:33–39
Ephesians 1:4–5
Philippians 1:6
1 Thessalonians 1:4–5
Hebrews 10:19–23
Hebrews 11:1
1 John 5:13

Repentance
1 Samuel 7:3
Ezekiel 18:31–32
Matthew 3:1–8
Matthew 4:17
Luke 15:7, 10
Luke 19:8–9
Acts 2:37–39

Repentance
(continued)

Acts 3:19–20
Acts 8:22–24
Romans 2:4
2 Peter 3:9

Suffering
Book of Job
Psalm 43:2–3
Psalm 50:15
Psalm 107:26–31
Psalm 112:4–8
Psalm 119:71
Romans 5:3–5
2 Corinthians 1:5–11
Hebrews 10:32–35
1 Peter 2:19–21

Worry
Psalm 94:19
Psalm 139:23
Ecclesiastes 2:22–24
Matthew 6:25–34
Matthew 10:19–20
Philippians 4:6
1 Peter 5:7